J332.024
Sch   **DATE DUE**   2/16

APR 2 3 2018			
			PRINTED IN U.S.A.

MONEY MATTERS

Spending Money

by Mari Schuh

BELLWETHER MEDIA • MINNEAPOLIS, MN

Note to Librarians, Teachers, and Parents:

Blastoff! Readers are carefully developed by literacy experts and combine standards-based content with developmentally appropriate text.

Level 1 provides the most support through repetition of high-frequency words, light text, predictable sentence patterns, and strong visual support.

Level 2 offers early readers a bit more challenge through varied simple sentences, increased text load, and less repetition of high-frequency words.

Level 3 advances early-fluent readers toward fluency through increased text and concept load, less reliance on visuals, longer sentences, and more literary language.

Level 4 builds reading stamina by providing more text per page, increased use of punctuation, greater variation in sentence patterns, and increasingly challenging vocabulary.

Level 5 encourages children to move from "learning to read" to "reading to learn" by providing even more text, varied writing styles, and less familiar topics.

Whichever book is right for your reader, Blastoff! Readers are the perfect books to build confidence and encourage a love of reading that will last a lifetime!

This edition first published in 2016 by Bellwether Media, Inc.

No part of this publication may be reproduced in whole or in part without written permission of the publisher. For information regarding permission, write to Bellwether Media, Inc., Attention: Permissions Department, 5357 Penn Avenue South, Minneapolis, MN 55419.

Library of Congress Cataloging-in-Publication Data

Schuh, Mari C., 1975-
  Spending Money / by Mari Schuh.
    pages cm. – (Blastoff! Readers: Money Matters)
  Summary: "Relevant images match informative text in this introduction to spending money. Intended for students in kindergarten through third grade"– Provided by publisher.
  Audience: Ages 5-8
  Audience: K to grade 3
  Includes bibliographical references and index.
   ISBN 978-1-62617-248-7 (hardcover: alk. paper)
  1. Money–Juvenile literature. 2. Budgets, Personal–Juvenile literature. 3. Finance, Personal–Juvenile literature. I. Title.
  HG221.5.S378 2016
  332.024–dc23
                        2015006567

Printed in the United States of America, North Mankato, MN.

Table of Contents

Why Spend Money?

Why do people spend money? They use money to pay for their **needs** and **wants**.

COMMON NEEDS

food

clothes

school supplies

COMMON WANTS

games

toys

treats

People buy things they must have to live. They also spend money on fun things.

People spend money after
they get paid.

They also spend money once they reach a savings **goal**.

7

Sometimes people spend money when others need help. They **donate** money to **charities**.

People spend money when
their **bills** are due.

They pay for heat, power, and phone service every month.

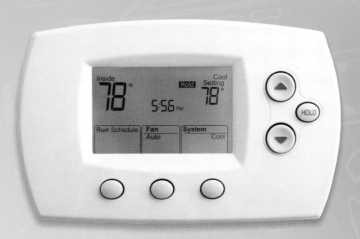

heat

power

phone service

Spending Money Wisely

People should pay their bills on time. Then they will not have to pay **late fees**.

ELECTRIC BILL

123 Streetname St.
Hometown, State
ZIPCODE

LOCAL HYDRO

BILLING NUMBER:	000**123**
BILLING DATE:	JAN 13, 2012
TOTAL AMOUNT DUE:	$88.46
DUE DATE:	JAN 30, 2012
PAYMENT ENCLOSED	

Please return this portion with your payment

CUSTOMER:

John Smith
456 Streetname St.
Hometown, Statename
ZIPCODE

BILLING SUMMARY: 000**123**

Previous Balance:
Total Payment
Balance forwar
Total Current U

ACC. 32

PERIOD: **NOV 26,**

Electricity supplied
Electricity **650.18** k
Delivery:
Regulatory Charges:
Other Charges:
Taxes:
Subtotal of electric C
Local benefit:
Total Electric Charge

221

Date: 2/9/2012 $ 88.46

Pay to the order of: Local Hydro
eighty eight dollars and 46/100   Dollars

John Smith

electric bill

Notes:

:726271621: 517379527 0221

$ 88.46

FEB-21-11
JAN-27-11
DEC-20-11

PAST DUE

88.46

TOTAL CHARGES:

TERMS ON YOUR STATEMENT

SERVICE: Local Hydro will supply all the electricity that the Customer needs for its home or business ("Supply Service"). Local Hydro is a retail marketer of electricity and not the Customer's Local Utility. The Local Utility will continue to deliver electricity to the Customer's home or business ("Distribution Service"), read the Customer's meter, bill the

Customer's service with Local Hydro will continue on a month to month basis until the Customer chooses to switch to another supplier and the Local Utility successfully changes the service.

RATE: Local Hydro offers a variable rate for electricity which may be adjusted on a monthly basis. Local Hydro may offer a one-time introductory rate for new customers which will be a term of up to three billing cycles. Following the term of the

People should try to pay their
entire bill. If they cannot, they
have to pay **interest**.

Buying things on **sale** helps people spend less money.

People also spend less money when they use **coupons**.

Credit cards
make spending
money easy.

People can use credit cards
too much. Then they **owe**
more money than they have.

Budgeting

Having a **budget** helps people plan ahead.

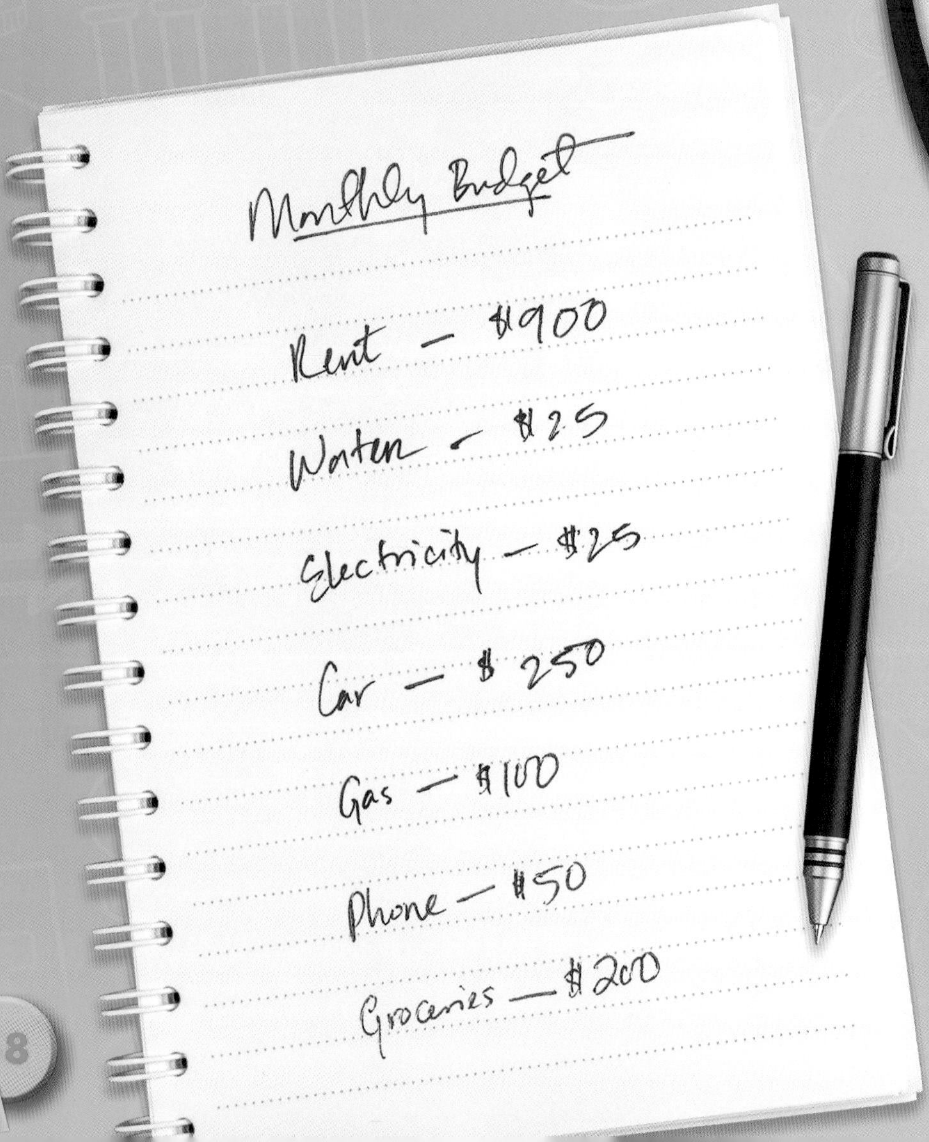

Monthly Budget
Rent — $900
Water — $25
Electricity — $25
Car — $250
Gas — $100
Phone — $50
Groceries — $200

Budgets list how much people will spend on different things, like food and **rent**.

| AD-Automatic Deposit | | AP-Automatic Payment | | ATM-Teller Machine | | DC-Debit Card | | T-Tax Deductibl |

NUMBER OR CODE	DATE	TRANSACTION DESCRIPTION	PAYMENT AMOUNT	✓	FEE	DEPO AMO'
001	5/1	Mortgage	$ 123612			$
002	5/8	Supermarket (food)	8751			
003	5/11	Electricity	12785			
004	5/16	Real Estate Tax	35917			

People keep track of how much money they spend. Then they know exactly where their money goes.

Having a budget helps people stay out of **debt**. It helps people be smart with their money!

Glossary

bills—written statements of money owed

budget—a plan for how money will be spent

charities—groups that raise money to help people in need

coupons—printed pieces of paper that let people buy things at cheaper prices

credit cards—plastic cards people use to borrow money to buy things now and pay for them later

debt—money that a person owes

donate—to give something away

goal—something that a person aims for or works toward

interest—extra money that is owed for borrowing money

late fees—money that is owed for paying a bill late

needs—things people must have to live, such as food, clothes, and a place to live

owe—to need to pay someone

rent—the cost of living in an apartment or house

sale—a time when items are sold cheaper than usual

wants—things people would like to have, such as games, toys, and treats

To Learn More

AT THE LIBRARY

Bullard, Lisa. *Kyle Keeps Track of Cash*. Minneapolis, Minn.: Millbrook Press, 2014.

Reina, Mary. *Learn About Money*. North Mankato, Minn.: Capstone Press, 2015.

Schwartz, Heather. *Spend Wisely*. Mankato, Minn.: Amicus, 2015.

ON THE WEB

Learning more about spending money is as easy as 1, 2, 3.

1. Go to www.factsurfer.com.

2. Enter "spending money" into the search box.

3. Click the "Surf" button and you will see a list of related web sites.

With factsurfer.com, finding more information is just a click away.

Index

The images in this book are reproduced through the courtesy of: Syda Productions, cover, p. 21 (girl);
dibrova, cover (left bills); sarahdesign, cover (shopping cart); martan, cover, p. 21 (dollar signs); Sergii
Korolko, cover, p. 21 (barcode); Robyn Mackenzie, cover, p. 21 (dollar coins, top right bills, pennies),
p. 21 (left bills); Zora Rossi, cover, p. 21 (sale sign); Vitaly Korovin, cover, p. 21 (price tag); Andrey
Popov, cover, p. 21 (cash register); lendy16, cover, p. 21 (fan of bills); Altin Osmanaj, cover, back
cover (bottom wallet); Brian A Jackson, cover, back cover (bottom coins); Monticello, p. 4 (food); Piotr
Marcinski, p. 4 (clothes); Sean Locke Photography, p. 4 (school supplies); Tashka2000, p. 4 (games);
LungLee, p. 4 (toys); Volodymyr Krasyuk, p. 4 (treats); Blend Images/ SuperStock, pp. 4-5; John Howard/
ExastoStock/ SuperStock, pp. 6-7; GrayMark, pp. 6-7 (money jar); Design Pics/ SuperStock, pp. 8-9;
Hellen Sergeyeva, p. 9; iofoto, pp. 10-11; Heymo, p. 11 (thermostat); Somchai Som, p. 11 (lightbulbs);
Pieter Beens, p. 11 (phones); Viktorus, p. 12 (electric bill); carmen2011, p. 12 (past due stamp); Mega
Pixel, p. 12 (checkbook); gchutka, pp. 12-13; Tetra Images/ Corbis, pp. 14-15; WendellandCarolyn,
pp. 14-15 (coupons); scanrail, p. 16; John Giustina/ Getty Images, pp. 16-17; Taweepat, p. 18; Fancy
Collection/ SuperStock, pp. 18-19; JohnKwan, pp. 20-21; dean bertoncelj, p. 21 (credit cards).